ecologue

ecologue

ken belford

HARBOUR PUBLISHING

Published by
Harbour Publishing Co. Ltd.
P.O. Box 219
Madeira Park, BC
V0N 2H0
www.harbourpublishing.com

Edited and designed by Silas White
Printed and bound in Canada

Harbour Publishing acknowledges financial support from the Government of Canada through the Book Publishing Industry Development Program and the Canada Council for the Arts, and from the Province of British Columbia through the British Columbia Arts Council and the Book Publisher's Tax Credit through the Ministry of Provincial Revenue.

Library and Archives Canada Cataloguing in Publication

Belford, Ken, 1946-
        Ecologue / Ken Belford. — 1st ed.

Poems.
ISBN 1-55017-349-9

        I. Title.

PS8503.E47E26 2005   C811'.54   C2004-907462-8

Acknowledgements

"Common knowledge," "Rats," "Food security," "Hats," "Land schemas," "Salmon," "The suicide economy," "The nervous system," "The journeyman" and "Remember, suppose, say" have appeared in *The Capilano Review*.

"Heterana," appeared in *The Literary Review of Canada*.

"The poetry class," "Noma, nama, nomen," "Corresponding divisions" and "All stalls" appeared in Rob Budde's web journal *stonestone*.

"Sublangual" appeared in the web journal *Reflections on Water*.

Contents

back talk

leaving andamayin: a sequence

living memory

The back talk song

I must have been diverted but
I don't remember where I was on 9/11.

It's not about the clown's silly toy
    or the flirt's perfect wiggle.
    It's not about the fool's fiddling,
        the tinker's twitch or
        the dabbling of the wand.

The back talk song's about
the reckoning of a culture
    that mostly favours proficiency
        and has no use for men like me.

Whenever missing a place to stay,
    when away from land –
    I pronounce the song of my home
    and say the names of the souls I knew.

They are carved into my walls
    and the bark of living trees.
From them I learned this song.

Weed book drift

Loggers wipe their asses with owls,
a synonym for the old growth.
But shit doesn't stick to feathers and
diversity is a moral responsibility
having to do with the transfer of properties.
Economists that neglect problems
choose ignorance and inaction.

Identity, by pointing on a map,
may be inaccurate.
We don't know much.
If we did we'd spend more
on replacing living things
than on buildings.

The process of temporary states,
including synonyms
for the elk of poetry
spreads like a Bitterroot Cascade
and is called invasion.

Invaders suck up more water,
transform and degrade community
and dirty vehicles spread
the order of magnitude.

By the number of appearances
on weedy lists, testing branches
name stabilized economic plants
and the present system spreads
on a continental scale.

Sublangual

Don't give up. There's help
like premature agreeing
and flushing gentries
in the paper.

Inflammatory spin
relives motion sickness
and double blond answers provide relief,
including the need to urinate at light.

For all the action with no reaction,
channel blockers are
a natural route to safer levels.

Today I took some placebo trails,
fallic acid and rad cells,
lucked into an illegal bear
and hit a fast-food drive-thru.

I aid in absorption.
I'm a proven wait-management product.
Trace stimulants need to reach homes.
Ask for more information.

Sequences

Anything is hung
  on the strings that run
    through the body

  and those who play on these
  are befuddled and befooled by lies
    until the fruit is disposed.

Likely given and prone to bend
  with head bent toward instinct
  I suppose that to follow in trust

  is the charity where conditions begin,
  where reticence creates backlogs
    with the odds on the runner

    who startles the snipe
    to flinch and bolt at dawn.

Living memory

Thin-skinned and wasted, I was fading.
  At the tip of my tongue,
    a creature of dissent
    spiked to a tree.
Unfit for work, with hammer in hand,
  I turned up at the end and together
    we drove the nails home.

And some went through and some did not.
Others were dull right out of the box.
Stuck in my occupation
  I was tired of fixing this to that.

As I got older I heard no stories
  from my family
  but I heard them in poetry,
    out of consonants and vowels of language.

Sniffing and snuffling, the breathers appear.
Hear my story, it isn't rewritten.

My mother calls me daughter.
I have families.
I hear the names of the land.
I don't live where I used to.

Hats

I'm walking downtown and it's minus 15.
I've got a hat for everything. I need my hat.
Coming up the hill toward me, an older man,
face battered, eyes me up. He's pushing a bike
and shoots me a look. I can see he's on the job
and looking for a break so we stop and talk
about men who know how to make things.

He's wearing an earflap skullcap, brain bucket,
reflective vest, work gear, good gloves and boots.
His bike's in useful shape.
And off the axle, a welded ball-joint bed frame
with modular plywood cart,
tiny cutting torch saddled onside,
everything right.

He's lugging a 30-gallon, glass-lined water tank
salvaged from a wreck downtown,
pushing it up the hill, living on welfare,
worked all his life, it's obvious.

Gives his finger to the Premier. He's working
for another, fixing houses for
the ones who didn't make the grade,
doing the real work.

Soak and dip

The rule is little and often:
don't wait and don't smother,
so that two surfaces can pass
easily over each other with a
minimum amount of friction.

Grinding wastes energy that
could have been used to move
you forward; you can get going
faster and sooner.

Hot parts
are at risk of damage and
seizing up so reduce wear.
Surfaces need a tough film
between each other, that way
they won't wear each other
down.

How much abuse do you
put it through? How often do
you use it? How often do you
clean up?

Grease the nipples
so they can turn in their seats.
Smear where the lines emerge
and drop a thin coat over it all.

Land schemas

The north moves north.
This song is an article of evidence.
Myths sustain the agenda,
    donuts are the fuel of ragers
    and fantasy is the glue.

    There's grime on the streets
        and I want to know how
        they got the dirt on me.

Most leaves don't touch
    but some appear to like it.
Power is against the good
    and I am a variant
        caught in a contradiction,
        modelled by another, needing to separate
    and grow distinct, to give up
    and go back to the bush
        where love's spongy congress gathers cause.

At first glance into the heavens,
I saw an unlikely elemental ancestry
    set in motion. The head and shoulders
    of a faceless charioteer drawn by stallion.

Who else but Pegasus could this be?
      So that I, the animal's husband
      would then know
      the stem of such descent?

My father farmed, his brothers too, his fathers too.
His hands husked chaff, instinctively he
      disliked weeds and this bad blood
      he saw was not his type and suddenly
            he was out of love for me.

There were fireflies in the pasture
      in the night and against the moon,
      multitudes of breeding and broody birds.

To confide in the earth is to bury,
      to whisper and shade,
      to hide in and cover with dirt.

Vessels are made of soil, mold, dust and clay.
Away in the burrow out of earshot,
      the earthworm snuffles toward connexion,
            an intentional conductor
            zeroing in on the return path.

Roadkill

Snakes bask in the middle,
birds eat the gravel,
mammals eat the salt,
deer eat the brush,
rodents live in the grasses,
songbirds bathe in the dirt,
moose travel along roads
and the scavengers get smacked
right in the centre.
Fragments are islands of trees
between clear-cuts.
These roads suck blood.
The better the highway
the worse it gets.

Salmon

Nearby and side by side,
they are not connected to you.
They are individuals, singular creatures,
earthlings like you.
Don't hound them with hooks,
pester or molest them.
Some are late and some are early.
Some are extinct and the rest are old.
They pour out of the ocean.
You can't send them back.
Believe in them.
Don't exaggerate their size or invest in them.
Forget reliance. All you can do is guess.
Don't agonize over them
when they beat their brains out.
You will put them off with your words.
They have no opinions or answers
and don't belong to you. They long for the depths.
Stubborn and irritable, they have no appetite or thirst.
They have faces and wear stripes.
The dogma of ascent means nothing.
Don't throw dirt on them.
Under the sun, in this world,
they stand on the bottom.

Take talk tag

I am it and the idea is
    to keep from being caught, then
    to overtake and touch.

    I'm the little bobtailed boy
        who follows a worthless word
           with a loose and ragged edge,
           tattered tail and matted hair.

Something's won today, something taken, something forced,
something sold, someone hired.
I want to take it away, take the photos back.

Someone took a wife today,
I took my chair and thought
    cars take people,
    ships take water.

I'm a combination, a takedown man
    who changed his mind.
I don't take exams,
roads take me to town.
The poem takes a beating, takes insults,
    has fever at dawn, is cold at night,
        understands deception, takes measures,
        begins again.

Rubbings

I was born twice over.
My father didn't take charge
and I showed up the second day.

Being is the idea of substitutions
and I'm a weary traveller
close to my parent star.

My family doesn't go back very far.
There's no line of succession.
They come from elsewhere.

I'm the secret sharer,
dirt means many things,
poetry turns to worms.

The house didn't do it.
I don't wear a suit.
My voice is flexible.

I'm not imprisoned in my family.
Survival is subject matter,
the clod, the ball, the egg.

Like them

It doesn't begin here but
    further down in the chain.

Last night I dreamed of great trout
    then first thing at dawn
        I Litton Monsanto
        and heard the fatherland's machines
        gunning their motors.

Men are the masters
    and the forest is the slave.

Language is the tool of occupation
    and this is the lingo of subsistence.
I don't win bread but I make it.
    Can't live without trout.

I'm not on the side of the bang.
The imperium is a tongue in the anus of science.
I don't do the Nabisco Sanyo Inco Stelco hip hop.
I'm not a quiet formalist.
Rolex you Mitsubishi!

I don't have a truck.
I'm not tired of working by hand.
I won't outgrow my shack
    and be like them.

My words cling to life.
I'm staying alive.
I'm going to outlive them,
    going to live longer.

On the loose

I get buried in dust
when I ride my bike

and that's why I don't like this
carousel of wrecks and shells

that rumble and whine
on these narrow local roads of the heart.

I'm in with the fumblers and botchers
the crackpots and loners

the men in the street
making ends meet

the guy on the rebound
the bozo, the dad

even the contagious clones of progress
making their calls in advance

when I'm on the loose
and take to the streets.

The living poem

This I know: the narrative of maps and dreams
others wrote on the outer walls
of my lover's heart imposes caution.

The righteous poetry of common meaning
doesn't do a thing for me
when I'm out in the badlands,
playing with your poodle, looking for
some compound-forming elements
and gathering inaccuracies
until the break of day.

I know the poem forms in the muck
until the compound stalk of love
influences the behaviour of animals
like me. I continued to grow
after my normal period.

I know words are next to the skin
and present in the body, I know
there's a crowd outside and a band inside,
a membrane bound organelle
way down in the deep,
that there's an assembly
outside and inside, another
rhythmic activity, a gathering.

Hot greens and cool blues

Forget the farm
and garden only a few things.
There isn't as much time as there used to be.
Move to town and live in the bowl.
Don't give away your car, shoot it.
Buy a bike and learn to care for it yourself.
Buy your food.
This is about hot greens and cool blues.
Live in a small home.
Cook your food quickly and never butter it.
Steam your vegetables
and brush them with olive oil.
Serve them.

All stalls

Can't get it out of my head.
Big farms are big mistakes.
Disease vectors.
Get ready to be a refugee.
Getting past free-market economies.
It's getting warmer but don't say it with flowers.
Past I'm.
Getting past perfect.
If it all stalls and the conveyor belts stop,
no more mining giants getting whole pigs.
No more getting by or even dead-end jobs.
Not even smash mobs jerking logs in the smog.
No more getting away or even getting out.
Get out, leave or escape.
Even better, help me out,
I've got it bad.
Don't cut it down, don't burn it up.
At least get somewhere.
Ready, dress, get up and grow. Equalize.
Take it in, turn it around, make it work.
Dirty old snow goes slow.
I've got to go.
Got rabbit in my DNA.

The nervous system

Fresh violence. There's a high risk
the guidelines worked out last night
᾽aren't in order today. As a rule,
payments are heaviest in the morning.

Systematically   The system's nervous.
It's all worked out
so that depending on
the length of the lineup
and the design of the set-up,
assessments are made, collected
and combined
into an orderly tax called style.

Mangled and bent,
screwed up, doctored and
distracted guy goes by

Distorted   making faces, muttering
twisted meanings.
Unlikely discordance:
hit or miss
dressed up deformity.

Listen to these accounts even if

Information   you don't understand them.
I'm an advance man. It's a fact.

Fragments in the looking glass

Driven back home,
  this is the other poem,
  the inconsistent one.

I've had enough and I'm spent but standing.
I didn't like your taste;
  two bodies sickened in a grim sideshow.

I didn't take your stinking, slimy, gooey bait
  and turned you down. This is a poem
  about survival and resistance.
It is scandalous and discordant.
This is a poem from the other side.
It is not accessible or simple or like anything else.

I wrote it before I ate. It isn't clear.
Critics are unwelcome here. I'm sick.
It doesn't resemble anything.
It's loose and unmuzzled.
No one will congratulate me for it.
It isn't about reality so you won't see
  your own world in this.
It isn't self-satisfied and smooth
  or even direct and full of rules.

It isn't truthful, literal, or substantial,
  not even practical or sensible,
  not mammal, bird, fish or reptile,
   it's tasteless. Suggestive and dirty,
  it's about smuggling.
I live in a place called buffalo
  where form is bewilderment.

The suicide economy

I was a poacher before I learned to be a guide.
I used to be a guide. There's still a fringe of land
away in the distance.

I don't know a thing about money
but I know I've been skimmed
by the supply chains.

To get a grip on it, make a fist.
To be happy, leave.

I had two gardens. The dark lords banned one,
fenced the other and called it procedure.

I'm not secure and I don't know a thing
about offshore servers so I write poetry
and keep my bees away
from corporate manoeuvres –
that way they can at least have a chance.

corresponding divisions

The kiss

There's no such thing as an innocent kiss.
An act to be considered and acknowledged,
a kiss endures, has consequences –
so if you must kiss me, kiss me on my eyes,
so close I can't see anything wrong.

The poetry class

The poem

Once I had a life.
I worked.
Now I don't know.
I've had to forget what I knew.

Before I was stolen
I was poor,
too poor to travel.

They took as many of us
as quickly as they could.
Now, countless slave poems below.
Now, no one wants us
and we have nowhere to go.

The poet

I learned poetry is a little bit late
because poems acquire relevance,
that poems aren't lazy,
that they take a long time
and that the class is a class.
Once I was an artist
and now I teach the poetry class.
I don't know.
It wasn't so good before.

Corresponding divisions

Mutant word: 123, 256.
Mistakes in the copy.
Marriage, version 2.1.
Separation was only half the solution.
Divorce finished the job.
Are rewired hearts too small to see
or hidden in the other forces of nature?

Saw heat waves turn off rain.
Didn't steal the food chain.
Needed a little more space
and got a little extra time.

Imagine this:
a simple model
built on
a two-dimensional surface
in three-dimensional space.

A poem isn't a dog
until it bites you
and becomes a story
that won't go away.

Noma, nama, nomen

At first I was known as Lew
and no one called me names.
I cut wood. I knew if it wasn't easy
it wasn't any fucking good.

Darlene was my dearest wish.
Some say I died but no one really knew.
Many great men were Lew
although Rob or Ken will do.

I'm not a namby pamby poet
with a namby pamby talk.
I never was an achievement slave
and then one day I slipped away

to make another name for myself
although it wasn't what you thought.
Noma is my first, Nama is my last
and Nomen's my assumed.

My namesake's Dick,
a self-absorbed emphatic man.
He's a somebody
and I'm myself.

The toggle switch

Suppose I made a wireless poem that said
since knowing you, since starting over,
knowing this love is the feedback loop
into the common currency, that
I've been stitching firefly words together
into a dream-time generator,
mem-brain sequencing,
inverting, dividing and surviving
with you, in the wild, ever since.
Suppose, suppose.

The journeyman

I'm a working class poet, a child of farmers.
I worked in the mills and sorted lumber.
I never taught school and I'm not celebrated.
Can't change that and can't change this.
There wasn't money to send me to school.
I know how to put up hay by hand, how to
make my handles, how to sharpen and
shape, how to join timbers. I lived where
scholars don't. Little is known of me. Only a
few are like me. I'm Canadian and the
author of these poems. I'm not invited to
read in the universities. They don't know
who I am. I learned to write in the middle
of the night after work was done. I'm thankful
we didn't have a bible. Nothing to read but
I knew I was a poet. None of us were
merchants, none studied the law, none the
healing arts. My father wanted to write. He
sold the farm and we moved to the city.
I found poetry there but I don't know how I
found it. I'll never be a sucky white boy.
I was 58 or 59 when I wrote this in 1741.
There were times I had no store food so I
lived from the land. I'm an unregulated voice
from the Nass. Alfred Purdy noticed me. I'm
ingenuous, have genius and I don't sing when
the harp comes around. Remember my name.
No one protects me. I owned my own boat
and made my own home. That's why poetry.

City limits

I'd rather forget the bush
I lived in, the old farm too.
The places I lived in aren't
gone yet but I've joined
something else now.

            I don't
believe in a mythic golden
age or the dominant view
so I collaborate in contexts
that don't close in on
themselves.

            I gained
more than I lost when I left.
Not for export, I remember
my place and mother tongue.
Reactions are not opposite
or equal.

            It wasn't Eden.
Mending is resistance and
going back is growing up.
As it happens I'm coming
around before progress
wipes me out.

Just one look at you

Remembering your shiny hair
 today I thought I saw you in a crowd
 and ducked away because
 I'm wild about another now.

You were an idea,
 a disorder I clung to
 and didn't want.
It's true I'm not ambitious
 and best at bringing up the rear.

Unbribed and true to my word,
 watching the sky for weather,
I was on my way to see the doctor,
 wanting to talk about
 the forming of opinion,
 blood relatives and allergies –

The busy disposition of the narrative,
 how happiness comes and goes
 and slips into omission.

Parallel worlds

Meaning waits in the unknown
and forests don't bounce back.

Doesn't matter what you think.

Turns out the closer you look
the more the poem unfolds

and since you can only move
forward or backward in a book,
poems appear one-dimensional –

although from a distance,

the separation of subject matter
from hard hats and safety boots
accelerates collisions in the background.

Homeopoetics

Performing animals die young.
They don't travel well
when being moved
from park to park.
Most have toys
in their stomachs.

Physical moments

Whenever an onstage dancer is rehearsing,
a shadow dancer is somewhere behind –
learning the dance, just in case.
It seems there's a turning point
when the director calls the women in.

Shadow dancers get the call after an injury,
or if the lead isn't good enough.
Or if she's tired and can't finish rehearsal
or falls and can't do the number.

She's had enough, the pail's full,
and she's happiest onstage
where she comes to life.
Backstage isn't interesting;
loves that don't mean much
other than the fatuous sense of feeling safe
for a few minutes in another's arms.
Whose arms doesn't matter.

There, she doesn't dance very well at all.
Her body seems heavy, it's too big
and her loves are addicts or drunks
like she is and now that she's old,
she's angry at the world, the way
things just don't seem fair.

Lingua

Trading tongues
by any means,

a rough and ready war
of word of mouth.

There's nothing to write home about.

Memory edit:
language is a dump.
I'm not at home in it.

Nothing's transparent
and resistance is referential.

The fix

It's a good idea to get used to
removing tightness so begin at
home. Things move out and
away from the rim: open and
release.

It's time for a refit
if you are banging around.
Tabs are there to give you time
to notice. Unwind a few turns
while learning how.

Change
gears, turn upside down,
remove slack, rest on ground,
strip and pinch around. Move it
in front of your lips and listen
until you hear it.

Everything
will be looser now. Repeat with
another until you figure it out.

Valentine's

Valentine's is past.
Drawn by lot, I was
a folded paper with a name inside
and for the next year
you had a plan for me,
an extravagant idea
that got to be too much.

Valentine pathways unite us
and fit our feet.
Hear the rings of our laughter.
The gathering continues
and we, by implication,
survive and breathe.

Between day and day I dream.
Last night a schooling salmon looked at me
and said in a matter-of-fact voice

    "First they got nervous about it getting late,
      then they piled up all over the place."

Then he squirted upstream,
leaving the freaks of a sentimental nature
to mate in the muddy languages
of common speech.

We began in the headwaters,
in the land and filth,
in the gossip, dust, slime and grime,
on the ground on which anything happens,
where the intervals of light
fall between one of us and then the other;
in the shadows of the old growth,
sheltered, saved and sustained
by hands we never knew.

Rats

(after Donna Haraway: an alien romance)

Freak scholars programming languages
    write in wannabe knowledge in Harvard.
In the academic-industrial complex
    the answer is yes and no.

For profit, Femanica drives
    rats to classes in her big, dirty car.
These creatures designed to suffer
    won't leave us alone.

Her Jesus is a dull rat
    and living memory isn't sentiment.
I want a chance to get a disease.
Go fuck gene therapy.

Caterpillars die in her veins.
Wouldn't touch a wild rat
but writes e-mail through
    a rat's brain in Nylon City.

Categories line up at the light
    where two-footed knowledge walks.
There are animals white men can't see.
Who is the gene genie that mothers the rat?

Hard-hatted men
    with the faces of wolves
    rip through the land on machines.
I like to write with the lights down low.
Stranger, certified being,
                    come into my home.

Food security

This is the potato that I worked so hard for,
that I walked to the marker for, that I paid for,
that I carried home in my bag, that I peeled
    and steamed the way you like it.
This is the potato you never ate,
so it sat on your plate
while you filled your face
with industrial shit
    in front of the TV.
This is the potato you blame,
    that I never ate again.

Detection

In the beginning, before the sorting of sounds,
    there was silence. Then the lords inserted master files
    named program and the user types
        at the command line put it into words.

Slave concept writers posted transmissions
in floppy diskettes until billions were at risk.

    When I filled in the password to begin
        an attemptress wearing the emperor's clones
        rode up on a house.

Give him your clothes she said
        and the memory resident files
            of my companion were deleted.

        I didn't know you were the enemy
    although already I was growing familiar
        with your threats and use of names.
Good thing I was turned off when I knew you.
Even better that I had a run priority.

        You are a common form
    of infectious memory waiting to open,
    self-replicating inbedding malicious code.
        I don't have a name for you yet,
        but you know, before too long, I will.

Landline

Hitmaking poems aren't served
until the Tinys reach American
brandstand. Power schools are
technically open when police
give homes the green light.
Accessing the light through
the second line, motorists wave,
lucky to get food. Summer
comes. Smog blankets the city.
I stood on a spit of land while
mother nature kicked into gear.
New tax dollars create more
temporary space beyond the
subdivision. The same ideas
still kicking around like sending
the buses to the people and
buffering parking clumps with
land parcels. Expensive stop
gaps and false promises don't
curb consumption. Trouble at
the top. Can't file an appeal
about arms racing either.
Request a benefit return, some
living memories and an empire
light to go. Neo-cons don't care
their spreading war is unreal.
Sing this voice print elsewhere
from the wired mice of Tampa.

Lines

shoot some botox
suck and tuck glam drug

into nerves around
age lines and

laugh lines vanish
when the nerves die

four in ten hardly breathe
want a new skin

double vision
say goodbye to wrinkles

get the fat from your ass
injected into your lips

scabs first, new skin below
talk out of your ass for real

The consumption of fair language

Birds in the bush
are better than one in the hand.

Meat is used vegetables,
a kind of shit made flesh.

The meaning of meat
is the word made flesh.

Some are out in trucks getting it.
Others are out in trucks distributing it.

On everyone's plate
the continuous recollection.

Memory rules: the body
and the renderings.

Text: subject and object.
Message as before.

Gravy costs extra.
Gravy over all.

Common knowledge

I'm writing by hand on the English channel
    because there aren't enough
    words to carry us.
    Used and unused waste flows through.

What letter spreads the word
    that first bruises shore with meaning
    then briefly slips away
    in the unstoppable flow?

Organs have common relationships
    and I, bearing a name others answer to
    am washed up with words,
    all over, done for now.

back talk

Homework

Power comes from doing things ourselves.
Power comes from generosity.
I'm a tributary.
Subsistence is my existence.
North or south, bush or city
makes no difference to me.
It's not the end when the economy collapses,
really it's just the beginning.
TV economics is hot air.
When you are away I cook,
when you're home I cook.
There's nothing new in what I do.
Life has to go on.
I don't give up.
Caring for the rich is a catastrophe.
Give me money and I'll get food.
Food is life.
I never worked a day in my life.
Homework isn't a grind.
The lord doesn't provide a thing.
The longer you work the sooner you die.

As if

It looks like rain and it sounds like a train is coming.
Since I'm in the mood for the unexpected
I think I'll have to run for it. Like father, like the devil.
I'm a deviant, a dissipated son.
I took a like amount of father's plaster
and wasted time. I cause delay.
Overnight I catch bugs.

These are hard times and I'm worthless and shifty.
I don't have an overcoat and my lining is a sheet.
I'm the table of contents, the index and errors.
I'm the dressmaker's model and my name is Joe Blow
but some call me Jack. As the one is, so the other is not.

Forget it

I made my home in another age, dreaming a habitat without a frame. Some people thought it was worthless because it didn't cost much but it took everything I had. I'm still a housekeeper and I don't want to get paid for it. Even back then I didn't do what I was told.

I learned to sharpen anything made to cut. The rest I made smooth. Out of the recurring old growth I ripped all the timbers, planks, shakes and boards I needed, accommodating the checks and rot in the great trees I lived in the shade of. I kept and caught no animals, made an income of my own and grew a few things.

I'm the voice from below. I pity the rich because they have so little. I'm not a socialist and don't own a condo or even a car. I don't see wealth and poverty the way academics do. I didn't ask for money, lived a good life and sacked a few delusions. In the south they are poor. I had land and didn't depend on money or an education, not even status and prestige. Didn't have agents and stood on my own feet. It's not natural to consume so much. What was good for me would be good for you. When I'm angry I imagine hunting trucks, the high ones with horns on their hoods. I live in another economy and it is both older and younger. My money isn't dead. I don't devalue my work. Forget it. I'm not interested in catching up.

Retouch

Circuits break and I believe.
What happens now
has never happened before.
Materials combine,
seamark is an unforgettable password,
four quarts make a gallon
and I'm a paper maker. I arrange lines
and get along with the available.

At the moment of comprehension
you gathered up and tasted my hand,
grazing old injuries,
in contact with sympathetic memories.
I thought of tidal flats, natural boglands
over which recurring waters flow.

Love is an unforgettable password
and I'm a volunteer.
Make nothing of it if you wish
but as far as I'm concerned,
love completes the circuit.

At 58 I went to my desk
on Blackwater Lake
and thought about love, the kind
that knocks you right on your ass.
You flew back to Prince George
and I went to my tent.

At 58 I went to my desk
and took out a paper and wrote
I love you and looked out
over the lake and across my life
and thought about farewells.

Tape measures

Winter sere –
trees, lights, wrap.

You – 50-percent-off price.
Mattress sets on floor,
the bread sticks. There's more
than I came for.

The merchandise returns
when the black and white mixer
substitutes that old hand tossed deep-dish order
for a cheesy delivery.

Folding leaves brighten any room
and styles vary by location
provided you comply with the rules.

The perfect crack-pot idea
for the wireless remote
off-road family
upsized to large.

Not a

I'm not a slave to the doc, or a
slave to work. Not a slave
to sickness in the republic of
porkdom, not a money grub.

Not to making you better or to
cotton pants. Not to news, or
the muse, not the states, not
family, meat or the elite.

Not the city, pity, love, the
poem, home or drugs. Not
George, not Dick. Not heads,
head. Not cows, cowbells,

last calls, blue balls, not pets,
vets, hot bets. Not cooks,
guidebooks for secret places,
barbed hooks, rushing brooks.

Not more, less, not bills, pills,
stalls, malls, bare hills, knew
a river in the forest, saw
big systems rolling through.

Life sentence

Kurdish firefighters are still battling mud. Car goes to the United States. Perpetrators higher up ask if life means life. Looking for volunteers, heads of state pour into the streets. Forest fires in Gitxsan territory. In Marseilles, youth were arrested and given a life sentence. Robust forces back right off and get out of town. Troops need better protection. Trial chambers are serious cases that reflect gravity. Land mines kill reconstruction. Salvage crews clear the way while victims seek a heavier sentence. Groups take over the end.

Languages, stray cats

When looking back, the obsolete lie. A snare on stick. Making my cingulate journal. What's missing is a place to stay. Heading back to square one. There's no such thing as black and white but a burgundy middle. I don't like these politicians who don't like themselves. I don't like these instant shamen. I don't like this plastic furniture that doesn't have a particle of soul. I don't like the work they make us do so I compose outside the margins. I don't like motivational seminars. Better happy than rich. I don't like these cotton clothes that kill rivers. For every story that's told, another's suppressed. I don't like these best-selling books that guarantee more trade goods. America's democracy is a passing fad. Preaching work and purchasing, that's how the world is run. The basic lessons are forgotten. They sit on their asses in classes but don't educate the soul. Students have learner's licences and want to fill up on credit. Labour-saving devices escalate the suicide economy and labour-saving tools don't leave scuz. Any way is okay so long as I get there, on time, home, home again, where I live. Like obstructions in the mind, sugar-coated sentences or meaty excess, dope's in the news. We think we need some dope. Loaded with desire we face the TV and eat industrial junk. Let's do something that doesn't involve eating. Treat my sores, raw word.

Radicle

I was born before
status inflated headstones,
before houses belonged to
the others who wrote about things.
I didn't have anything to do with it.
My tongue twists along the river.
It's different this time.
This was written before I was born.
It's about water.
I'm not the go-to person anymore.
Decisions are not always efficient or quick.
One person, one decision.

My ground is going.
I don't shape solutions,
didn't fill the harness
and took my place in line
with the blind and the shot.
Serious debate ends when fatigue takes over.
Leadership characteristically follows
so many distractions.

Code

In America there is a school of thought that says
you have to get there first.

Most of us need the company of others
and America has more empty places than ever.

But if you scratch the surface behind the love marks
you will find the program is the product

and the merchandise is the narrative
of loyalty beyond reason.

America I'm tired of paying more for less and I've lost my faith.
Your advertisements are like roaches –

I spray them and spray them and they keep on coming
because the persuaders in the holding companies

build on the need for mystery and meaning
by keeping the story believable.

Heterana,

Some of us are we and some are they;
a generation subject to another's rules.
Bearing flowers that are of two kinds,
at variance with doctrine, I split into
two halves. The fingers of my left hand
open outward into rings.

                    On the other
side of the page, lines diverge. There
we write one thing and mean another.
A glimpse of salmon squirting around
the city. Grabbing and loading up on
them is non-adaptive now.

                    Snatching
words, never put your iron hand on me,
never develop, snag or net me. Your
glassy eyes, your far-fetched narrative,
your vacant face.

                    Before vowels, when
nouns were hybrids and had more than
one stem, warmth was the miracle and
awe the fire.

Remember, suppose, say

We got more than we asked for
when we turned back the clock.
This is a story about detail,
about how some loves cool and collapse
as they expand.
The idea takes getting used to
but it all started
in the form of an unexpected correspondence
from across the valley.
Nothing explains it
but I closed the door and walked away
until I couldn't be seen anymore.
What happened, what force,
what dark energy?
What was going on
before everything stopped working?
In the afterglow, the encoded information
of those early days raises new questions
about getting around
problems like remembering the question
and getting the last laugh.
I did good work back then,
in the beginning.

leaving andamayin

: a sequence

(leaving Andamayin

Adaptable and dirty, I lived
thirty years here and thirty there

in floods or a flood, numbers or mountains,
outsmarted and swarmed –

and many's the time
and many the people,

a no account,
a mapless mapper

I went one day
with one too many.

(before now

I wanted to stay
but days before ice

with fish in great numbers,
par para par

growing by chance
in the moss,

in the ground,
in the bogs,

in the trees
and the stones

making the most,
most of them missing.

(the curve

No hero(n)s
here, no simple parts.

Could you flow like me
you'd turn around.

Fair at six, going out at seven,
I felt the river lift and surge.

The holding water faded and
pack force isn't mob rule.

Crowded around soft dirt,
jams crush the corners.

The laws of their combinations
cannot be known.

(the river

And I can keep the secrets
of the mysterious places
on the other side
meant to be kept unknown.

Eight miles long,
it seemed more than that.
A long river,
never tedious
like lists or meetings,
it reached backward
into time,
a friendship I can't forget.

(against the yarn

Long ago, when
sheds were used more
and not these empty places,
before I went away,

something crossed
above me. A stone lifted
off the bottom
and began rolling in the riffle.

I heard it clicking
on the bottom, rolling by,
rolling through the curve, until
it found another place downstream.

Nothing lasts long.
Oh tributary, waterway, wandering path.
Rocklike rule, wobbly crutch.

Deceived and swindled
of my hard work,
I'm like you.

(leaving

I'm not that kind of I.
Filled up to here
with raw memories,
sedimentary fatigue
and bright water,
I left today.

The rubbed, ruddy bark
of the stems and root balls catch
same place, where the dead go.
This is what happens.

(leave your stick here

I'll give you a hand
but I'll need the other for balance.

The banks are undercut
until trees fall into the river,

then their trunks turn the water
outward to the bend.

In Eden there are more than enough trees.
When the river surges, everything moves.

(crossing

Here's the margin where
other living beings cross to go around.

I'm not too distant and I don't live in the city
so I can't forget the places or the stories.

Even in a go-between it's not possible
to find a street in the exposed particular.

Are academics invader species?
What's as watery as thawing mud?

I learned to cut but didn't divide the land.
Didn't cut it down, didn't reduce wages.

Couldn't go quickly,
just wanted to go.

(two lines cut

Don't want to hear those half-assed poets
and their stories of the farm.

Got off the sable fable too. Can't do
the agony of animals anymore.

Here the river cuts a new channel.
Don't need to rip lips or chew on wild ribs.

(distal love

I'm a single-seeded fruit
cycling through.

Small piece of meat and flat cake
of crumbs, hollowed out
ready-made discount love,

I won't stick my tongue
into your large sucking mouth.

In this alphabet
you are a parasitic larva,
a sac containing morbid matter.

(in other words

You wanted too many
seasons' work from me

and when I wasn't faithful
to the original reason,

when I moved
from one to the other,

as in the possessive and
double possessive case of you,

there was a gain
and there was a loss –

and you, a thin-blooded person
with a sour smile,

were lost in translation
somewhere between

my fictional character
of little depth and width

and a rhetorical device
used predictably.

(gnosis

Unnumbered and one of the rabble,
my father's name was fella.
Behold the butter and egg man,
what he did and what he didn't.

Scuttle when you see me miser.
I'm the best friend of the Blackwater,
watchman and frequenter of the river.
I stood guard here half my life.

Muddled, jumbled, distressed
and beaten by teachers,
I came here on short notice.
Some say too soon, others too late.

Today my debts are cancelled
and no one confines me.
Music goes with the words.
I'm going, too, and not too fast.

(fictorious plasma

I have long gashes and my lining is exposed.
For half my life I made meaning, pleased and taught;
a drudge held as a kind of property bonded to the land.

No roads here, never was, never will be.
About to be struck by something flat, I switched
from the tame and got out of the way.

My husband was a beggar, my wife a preacher
so I heard my share of whining and droning.
The trail fit my feet going back and forth.

Going is better than coming. Some say I disappeared
somewhere between a fable in the old growth
and a roaded narrative of simian drivers sleeping it off.

I won't be back and I'm inclined to say
all the trees are falling, that I'm not a slave
of stimulus and unafraid to travel on my own.

(baffle island

Today I passed through Customs,
    the language barriers, the bad bargains,
        the disturbing thoughts and soundtracks,
        through the lines of separation

    and through the gaps, wounds and stitches
    of beaten souls grouped together in a line.
Now any outdoor fire on rising ground
    at the water's edge could be mine.